PRACTICAL YURTS

Building and Living in a Low Cost
Alternative Structure

STEVEN W. HATCH

ISBN: 1496089995
ISBN 13: 9781496089991
Library of Congress Control Number: 2014904066
CreateSpace Independent Publishing Platform
North Charleston, South Carolina

CHAPTER 1

MY SITUATION

My name is Steve Hatch. I am 60 years old. Now living in a yurt in Portage, Utah. This book is about my journey into my yurt. I thought this book would be useful to others because I had many questions and finding the answers was not easy. This resulted in a lot of anxiety and frustration. Hopefully, you will find the answers to these questions helpful and you can see your pathway into a yurt of your dreams.

Yurts can be the answer to some people who are having a housing crisis. They offer a less expensive way to get into a house and have the independence that we often desire. A mortgage can be a strict taskmaster, one with little forgiveness.

My journey started on April Fools Day, of all days. Maybe this was an omen, who knows. After working at my job for 36 years, I was laid off and suddenly found myself without a job. This was a real challenge for me as my job had been a good one and had supplied me with everything I needed—plus a bit more than I needed honestly. I was not too stressed by money. For 36 years, every two weeks, a deposit was made into my account and I could mostly do what I wanted and the money was there within reason. I was not wealthy, but I was also not poor. I was comfortable.

Then my situation changed. It all started a couple of years before when I was divorced and lost my big house on the hill. I was one of those who bought when the price of homes was high, and sold when the price of homes was low. I bought in 2006 at the height of the housing bubble and sold in 2011. Without my wife's income, I couldn't make the payments on the mortgage. This cost me a lot and left me renting an apartment.

Fast forward to 2013, and I was living in this apartment when I found myself unemployed. Rent was expensive and I knew that I needed to make some changes. I couldn't go on financially. I was seeking a job, but not having any luck.

I had been looking at land for sale for some time on the online classifieds, hoping to find some land to move onto because I wanted to move out of the apartment. It was a nice apartment, but apartment living was not what I wanted long term. Now, the pressure to move mounted. Rent and insurance! These were the big items that needed attention. Cobra coverage was expensive and there was nothing I could do about that.

So, that left the rent. I had signed a rental agreement that was due on October 1st—I would either have to renew for another year, or move out! That gave me six months to find some land and build a new home. That or find a home on the market that I could afford.

I looked at the real estate ads for homes for sale. The price of homes was well out of reach of the amount of money that I could muster. I was old, out of work, and getting a mortgage was out of the question. With all my calculations, I figured the most I could afford was $60,000. This had to buy a place for me to live and a place for my horse. I needed a place in the country. I looked at lots of property, maybe as many as 75-100 different offerings. It was a trying time and I finally found a piece of property here in Portage for $18,000.

It was one acre with animal rights. It had an old barn and corral for my horse and was connected to the city water system. That really solved one of my big problems, which was how to get water on my property. Many other properties would have required me to dig a well. As you know that is not cheap and also a bureaucratic mess to get the well permit, unless someone had already gone through the hassle of getting it before you bought the property. Here in the desert, water is a big issue.

After getting the water and property settled it was early June and I was hoping to get right on it! I had $42,000 left in my budget. I was now committed to moving out of the apartment before October 1st. As it turned out, I would actually move out on October 16th, and I did not have my yurt up yet. It actually wouldn't be up until November 6th.

While all the paperwork was getting prepared and in order, I built a small, 10 ft. diameter yurt, mainly to understand how to build yurts. I ended up living in it for over a month. It was surprisingly easy to live in and I learned a lot about yurts in the process. It is now used as a small storage shed, but for a while it was home. In this picture, you can see my lot, the small yurt under construction, and my horse trailer.

Winter came early and cold this year. It was down in the 0 to 10 degree temperatures at night late in October and into November. The little yurt was heated with a 1500 watt electric heater. I slept on a cot with a sleeping bag and a wool blanket on top. I was able to be snug as a bug in a rug in that little yurt. The only hard thing was going out to the outhouse to use the bathroom in the middle of the night when it was so cold.

I had a one of those water coolers that you put the 5 gallon jug of water on top. It had both hot and cold water, so I was able to have hot water for a cup of Pero and Cup of Noodle soup. I was also able to have a nice cold drink when I wanted to quench my thirst.

I had put in some shelves and had a pantry with canned goods, and stuff, as well as a place for my luggage, where I stored my clothes. I put my dutch oven and dutch oven cooker outside the door, so I was able to cook meals. It is possible to really shrink your living space and get along ok. I spent $700 on the small yurt.

Now, onto why I chose a yurt.

CHAPTER 2

WHY I CHOSE A YURT

You have a total of $42,000 to buy a house. What are you going to do? What are the options you have available?

1. Stick built home

2. A modular mobile home

3. A monolithic geodesic dome

4. A Yurt

There are other options I am sure, but these are the 4 options I looked into. So, starting with the stick built home. Most of the homes that contractors were building and selling were over $200,000. The low end homes were in the $150,000 range and it went on up from there.

My previous home, a 4500 square foot home was built for $345,000. This included the price of the lot. Lots in town were selling for a minimum of about $50,000 for a half acre lot in town with no animal rights. Most lots were selling for around $75,000. These lots are in a subdivision where the water and electricity are available in the street. The developer had put in curb and gutter, sidewalk, and the roadway. The lots around me at the big house were asking $120,000.

So lots like this were not going to be affordable. Now that I had made up my mind that I couldn't buy a lot like this and build on it, I needed another way. I looked at properties up in the mountains, where some lots were in the $35,000 range, but the water issue would have taken a lot of money. It would cost around $45 per foot to drill a well, and in addition I would have to buy the pump, the down pipe, and storage tank at the surface. Sometimes well permits are hard to get if the neighbors protest the well—often fearing another well would lower the water table and make their well go dry.

My son and I sat down and planned out a 24 x 24 stick built house and what it would cost. We estimated that if we did the work ourselves and just had the material costs, we could maybe get it into the $40,000 range. We were looking at things very optimistically. If anything didn't go per plan, we would go over budget. Also, it was a very plain box structure. I was concerned that it was too plain and it didn't express my personality. Also, looking at the estimates we made and what it did end up costing me to put in the yurt, we were very optimistic. For example, the septic tank cost twice what we estimated.

Originally, I was looking at building a log cabin. I could buy a log cabin kit for about the $40,000 price. As I approached the building inspection department to understand more about the building permit requirements, I found out that a log cabin fell into the stick built home category from a permitting perspective. This meant that the walls had to be R30 and the ceilings had to be R45. To get those kinds of insulation values, I had to go to a log house with much larger logs, or they would build a log cabin and insulate it and put log siding on to cover the insulation.

Another thing was to build a log cabin with double log walls. That way you could insulate between the walls and meet the requirements. These structures were all outside of my price range. So I had to look at the next alternative.

A modular home—double wide—was the next option. I went to the modular home dealer and found out that I could buy a modular home for $69,000 but by the time, I added the foundation and transportation, the cost was around $80,000. In addition, the insulation was R30 in the walls and R30 in the ceilings. I told them that the county required R45 in the ceilings. They said, yes, they could do R45, but that would be a special engineering design and custom fabrication—all of which added cost to the already too high price.

I was discouraged, but this piece of information ultimately led to the solution. I asked them how they were able to sell them with only R30 insulation values, as it was obvious that they were being sold. They couldn't explain it, so I was left to wonder.

I went back to the building inspection department for the county and asked how the modular homes were being allowed in with only R30 in the ceilings. The answer was,

"Modular homes are not controlled by us, but by the Federal Government (HUD)."

So, my mind started thinking,

"Different types of structures are controlled by different codes?"

This was the thought that ultimately let me build my yurt. Yurts are controlled by a part of the code for alternative structures—membrane covered frame structures.

Modular homes were out because the cost was too high. So, this left the option of a monolithic geodesic dome home. These are some very unique structures in that they are built around an inflatable form. You pour your concrete floor and then place the inflatable form on there and blow it up. It takes the shape of the dome. You go inside and spray a urethane insulating foam on the inside to a certain thickness. Then you put in rebar, both horizontally and vertically around the dome. You also put in the electrical system wiring around the perimeter of the interior, for outlets, lights, etc. After this, you spray the inside with shotcrete, a form of concrete that can be sprayed. When the concrete sets up, you have a very strong structure. This is a very brief overview of monolithic domes and if interested you can research them on the Internet.

While I was looking at land, I met a landowner who was also living off the grid. He had built several of the monolithic dome homes, for himself and others. He had all the spray equipment and stuff to build the dome and even offered to help me build it. However, the land I was looking at had some accessibility problems with a right-of-way. I decided against buying that property. Also, as I talked to the guy I found the costs were similar to a stick built home and I felt that I wasn't able to afford to build it. It was a very interesting thought and was seriously considered.

That left me with a yurt. It was appealing to me from an aesthetic point of view. I got the book, *Living in the Round*, by Becky Kemery. This was a very important book in my journey, for two reasons. One, it influenced me greatly to appreciate what I could do with a yurt, and secondly, it was useful in getting my permit because I loaned it to the building inspectors, which allowed them to see that there were people building and living in yurts all over the country. I highly recommend this book to anyone considering a yurt.

In Becky's book, there was a quote from a builder who builds frame panel yurts, which are a form of yurt that is more like a stick built home. He described having open houses for his buildings and having people comment on the "feeling" inside the yurt. He indicated that on the regular rectangular homes he built, he would get comments on how nice the home looked, etc., but he didn't get the emotional response that he got when people visited his yurts. People talked about the feeling inside the yurt.

I had experienced this feeling too. One winter, I went into Yellowstone National Park by snowmobile to Old Faithful. The park in the winter is fantastic. I recommend that you take this opportunity if you get it! Anyway, at Old Faithful, they had some yurts setup for people to warm up in after their snowmobile ride. I went in them and was mesmerized with the feeling that I had while in them. Not only did I get warm—it felt nice to be in them. They seemed much bigger on the inside than they looked on the outside. This still amazes me!

Also, living in Utah in the winter is skiing time. People, from all over, come to Utah to enjoy the snow, especially the powder snow. Some of the ski resorts have yurts set up for skiers to get in out of the weather. They are also available for groups to use for family gatherings, etc. This way a family has a private place for food and clothing during the day. Mothers can spend their time in the yurt while the kids and cousins are all up on the slopes. The yurt becomes a central hub in the day's experience. I had been in, and used the yurt at Beaver Mountain Ski Resort, so I knew what they were like. There are yurts on top of the mountain at Park City, Utah.

In Park City is a unique restaurant. It is up at 8000 feet altitude and to get there the patrons ride up in a sled. The yurt serves food along with some entertainment. It is so popular that they have added a second yurt to their business.

Also, there are several backcountry yurts set up for cross country skiers who like to ski into the backcountry and stay overnight in a warm shelter. All these experiences with yurts had given me a vision of what could be.

Another feature of the yurt that is appealing to me is the dome. It seems to be the focal point of where you look when you walk into a yurt. It also lets in the light. I love how light it is inside the yurt during the day. The skylight lets in lots of natural sunlight and it makes the yurt feel good. Also, with a yurt, it is interesting to follow the sun around the walls. It is like you have a built in sundial. You can always know about what time it is by where the sun is shining on the wall. At night on a full moon, the light shines in and creates a beautiful spot of light on the floor or the walls. I enjoy the full moon from inside my yurt. Lying in bed looking out at the stars lets you know it is clear. You can tell when the clouds come and hide the stars. This is another little reason I love my yurt.

When I priced out my yurt, from Rainier Yurts, in Tukwila, Washington, I found I could buy the yurt with all the options for slightly over $30,000. This would leave me about $10,000 to build the base beams, buy appliances, install the septic tank and electricity. Shipping from Washington state to here was $2850.

This fit into my budget and was pleasing to me from an aesthetic perspective. I was also told it could be put up really quick and I was thinking this was what I needed because I had to be out of my apartment by October 1st. I hope you can make sense of my thinking. I could live in my yurt without a mortgage, on my own land, and room for my horse. I am planning on creating my little homestead on this property with my garden and the things I need to be more self-sufficient.

CHAPTER 3

PLANNING AND PREPARATION

The planning and preparation phase started when I moved into the apartment. I started looking for property. I knew that the apartment was temporary and that I needed something suitable for me. Many of you who have lived in apartments know what I am talking about. There is the noise of others and then you are trying to be quiet so as to not disturb your neighbors too.

So, I was looking in the classified ads online and in the newspaper. When I got the chance I would drive and check out various properties. The criteria that I was using was the following:

- One acre minimum

- Animal rights

- Access to water and electricity

- Rural, yet not too far

CHAPTER 3: PLANNING AND PREPARATION

Once I had selected my property in Portage, I needed to get my building permit. I went to the county building inspection department and asked what I needed to do to get a building permit. They gave me a checklist of things that I would need to do.

1. I had to have a plot drawing, showing the property and the planned location of the house. It had to include all the setback requirements, location of utilities, etc. Where was I going to get those? What form did it need to be in? Blueprint? Computer drawing? Hand drawn?

2. I had to have a sewer permit from the Health Department. How do I do that?

3. I had to have a layout drawing of my floor plans and an elevation view? Did I need to hire an architect?

4. I had to meet the 2009 International Residential Building Code. How was I going to do that?

5. I had to meet 30 pounds per square foot snow load on my roof. Part of engineering package

6. I had to meet the seismic standards. Part of engineering package

7. I had to meet the wind loads of 90 mph. Part of engineering package

8. I had to pay my fees. Who do I pay them to? How much?

9. I had to meet the insulation codes.

You can see I ended up with lots of questions. They said the place to start is the Town of Portage Planning and Zoning Committee. So that is where I started. I introduced myself to my neighbor and asked about the Planning and Zoning Committee and when they met. I went and asked them all the questions that I could think of and then started working on the answers. They gave me a paper that had all the setback requirements and things that they needed.

I feel that working with the Planning and Zoning Committee in a small, rural area was helpful to me getting my permit. I think one might have more difficulty in a larger urban area. I don't know that for sure, but that is my feeling. The people in Portage were of the opinion that if it doesn't interfere with anyone else, and it is what a person wants to do, then let them proceed. They were very easy to get along with.

The Town of Portage also needed the plot drawing showing the location of the house, and showing it met the setback requirements. This was one of the things I needed for the building permit, so I sat down and made a hand drawing on a piece of 8.5 x 11 standard paper.

I went through the process of choosing what kind of house I would be building, as discussed earlier. By this time it is late June. I drew in the yurt and the setback distances. I filled out the building permit form for Portage. I took my documentation to the July Planning and Zoning Committee meeting and presented my plans, the plot drawing, and some pictures of yurts and the interior layout of the yurt. The Planning and Zoning Committee approved it and now I had to take it to the county. But first, I had all the other things on the checklist to do.

So, I started working on the engineering package. I called Rainier Yurts, the supplier who supplied me with my yurt, and asked them about the engineering requirements. They told me they had an engineer that could do the work for me, but it would be a custom site plan drawing and site-specific engineering package. So I paid the fee and got the engineer working on that problem. The package was completed and delivered in August. The engineer did a very thorough job of designing the yurt to meet the codes and his analysis was very well documented. The building inspection people were completely satisfied with the work that was done by the engineer. The yurt met the wind requirements, well actually exceeded the requirements. It is good for 95 mph wind loads. The yurt met the seismic requirements, and exceeded the snow load requirements by 3 pounds per square foot (33 pounds per square foot).

One of the problems that perplexed me was how was I going to deal with the cold winters here in northern Utah. There will be at least two weeks every year where the temperatures will never rise above zero degrees. It is common to experience 20-30 degrees below zero. I was worried about my pipes freezing, both the incoming and my drain pipes. How could I protect the p-trap from the tub from freezing? How could I keep the water line coming in from freezing? Would I have to build a basement and bring them in below the frost line? If I built a basement, then I would need a sewage pump to pump the sewage up into the septic system, which is only buried 30 inches deep. How much would that cost?

The Planning and Zoning Committee said that the water line needed to be buried at least 4 to 5 feet deep to prevent freezing. I actually ended up burying it 5 feet deep, since that was how deep the city water line hookup was buried.

I worried about this for a long time. I tried different designs that had the plumbing in a separate small stick-built addition on the side of the yurt. I thought of building a basement and putting the yurt on top of the basement. All this would cost extra money. This complicated the engineering and would require a separate architect to design that portion. This was a big concern.

I worried about this for the whole time and even after I had made the decision to go the direction that I went. I was not certain that I was going to be all right. Here is the decision that I made.

I elevated the tub by 9.25 inches (the width of a 2x10 board) and kept the p-trap inside the building where it would be heated and at room temperature. So I built a platform in the bathroom to do this. It turned out to be really nice and I like the way it is. I can sit on the platform when I am cleaning, or otherwise in the bathroom.

This made the drain pipes go straight into the septic tank and we put a good slope on them so they drained quickly into the tank. The tub, toilet, washing machine, sinks, everything just drained out quickly with all the p-traps inside the yurt. We have had 20 degree below zero weather and so far it is working great.

The incoming line I brought up out of the ground from a 5 foot depth and up into the yurt inside the bathroom walls. I wrapped it with heat tape. The platform for my yurt is 30 inches off the ground so the pipe is exposed for this distance. Actually, a little more than this because is comes up at an angle. After wrapping the pipe with heat tape, I wrapped the heat tape to the pipe with a 200 degree rated tape (3M duct tape) per the instructions with the heat tape. I then wrapped the whole thing with fiberglass insulation and taped it around the pipe as well. I ran an outlet with a GFCI breaker on it down under the yurt next to the pipe and plugged the heat tape into that outlet. This also has been working.

So, no basement, just a nice platform made out of SIP (Structural Insulated Panels) flooring that came with the yurt. It was an option and I ordered it that way.

The sewer permit was next. I went to the Health Department and they gave me a checklist of things to do to get the sewer permit. Many of them were already done, like the plot map. I paid my fees and thought everything was going to be ok. A couple of weeks went by and I started wondering and getting nervous about what was going on at the Health Department.

I went to check what was up and they had misplaced my paperwork and so I had to resubmit. This I did and they responded quickly to help me get going again, but nothing could bring back the two weeks.

The first step in getting the sewer permit is digging a test hole. This hole has to be 10 feet deep. So I hired a backhoe to come dig the test hole. I did it on a day that the Health Department engineer could be there to witness it. The backhoe dug down 10 feet and the engineer made some measurements, noting the soil types and depths. Then the backhoe operator covered the hole back in and it was done. It took about 30 minutes to complete the test hole.

The Health Department then had to go do a preliminary design and give the data to me for getting the perc test (percolation test) done. A perc test is done by a certified perc testing guy. The Health Department tells him how deep to dig a hole, which is about 6 inches in diameter. Then he sets up his equipment and pours water in the hole and measures how long it takes to percolate down into the soil. He has to take readings every 30 minutes for 4 hours and then come back again 12 hours later and take some more measurements after the soil has saturated a bit. The readings have to fall within certain range of values in order to be acceptable.

Of course, you have to call one of the perc testers on the list given by the Health Department, and pay the fee for this test. This all takes about a week to coordinate and get done. The perc tester gives the data to the Health Department and they finalize the design of the septic system and give you a sewer permit.

The next step was the layout and elevation drawings. I took a chance, since the plot diagram was accepted as a hand drawn pencil drawing, and drew up my own layout plans. I was careful to do a nice job, so it wasn't sloppy and the writing was clear and legible. I did the drawings on 11x17 paper. They were not the blueprinted drawings that you would get from an architect, but then you didn't spend any money either. They were perfectly adequate for the building permit process. I took them into the building department and had them look at them to see that all the information was there and they approved them.

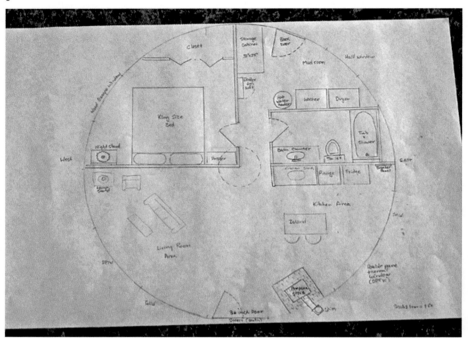

On the building permit, I had to have the names and license numbers of the contractors, like the plumber, electrician, etc. on the permit. I met with the plumber and showed him the layout and we discussed a rough order of magnitude cost. This then got the paperwork in order.

The only issue remaining was how was I going to insulate the yurt. The building inspection people were thinking it needed R30 and R45 and it wasn't going to meet that requirement. I printed out a blog, written by Dana Hendel of Rainier Yurts, that discussed the Radiant Barrier Insulation. I gave them my book, *Living in the Round*, by Becky Kemery for them to study.

I also directed them toward the portion of the code dealing with membrane covered frame structures, and let them work at their pace to study and approve the permit. It took them about a week and they gave me a call and told me my permit was ready to pick up.

After picking up my permit, I had to pay the permit fee to the Town of Portage. I was surprised with the size of the fee, over $1800, but then what are you going to do? That fee included a water system impact fee for a hookup to the city water system. I paid it and then it was time to start construction.

CHAPTER 4

BUILDING THE YURT

The first thing that I did to start the construction process was to locate the yurt on my property. I measured the setback distances from the street side property line and from the two side property lines. Since I had an acre, which was 188 feet wide by 252 feet long, rectangular, it was not difficult to get the proper setback distances. (For those purists out there, an acre is 43,560 square feet, and my property is actually 47,376 square feet, so it is slightly larger than an acre).

I chose the center point of the yurt and drove in a stake. Then I measured out the radius of the yurt, which was 15'2" in my case, since my yurt is 30' 4" in diameter. I laid these out in line with the four directions using my compass. I used a bright florescent orange string to stretch between all the stakes and this way I could visualize the yurt's footprint.

This was in the middle of August and I was thinking my deadline is really creeping up on me. Knowing that the money I would spend on rent for any additional time would be money that I couldn't spend on the yurt. I decided to build me a small yurt to live in if I had too and it could serve as a tack shed for my tools, saddles, bridles and stuff after the big yurt was finished. I also thought I would learn a lot about yurts to do this, which turned out to be true. In the photo below I have my rafters finished and I stood them in the position they would ultimately be placed in.

It is 10 feet in diameter and the walls are 60 inches in height. I built it out of 36 2x4x8 studs. I ripped 18 of them into fourths, giving me a 1.5" by ¾". This created the lattice wall. The other 16 were ripped in half to make the rafters and the other two made the door frame.

Here is the frame completed. I built the compression ring out of a single 2x8x8. I traced a 24 inch circle on some poster board and divided it into quarters. I traced one of these quarters on eight sections of the 2x8. Then I glued and screwed these pieces together overlapping the seams. Then I drilled the 32 holes at a 34 degree angle. This created the holes to insert the rafters into, which were then screwed in place to retain them in the hole.

I insulated the yurt with Radiant Barrier Insulation. I bought 40 yards of 11 oz. canvas and sewed the cover together. I painted the canvas after it was installed by outdoor latex paint to waterproof the canvas. This worked very effectively. By the time I was done, I had put $700 dollars into the small yurt.

This is the competed small yurt. This was what I lived in while completing my big yurt. I know it is a bit crude, but for my first project from scratch, I felt pretty good and it is very functional.

While I was building the small yurt, I was working on getting the septic system installed. After getting my septic tank permit, I contacted a reputable contractor to get a quote. I found out that it was going to cost a lot more than I wanted to pay, but I didn't know what to do. I was talking to another fellow who was building in town and he told me he got his installed for more than 35% less than the quote I had. I contacted this new contractor and he came and looked over the project and gave me a bid that was just like the other system he had installed. This was a great lesson in shopping around.

I had to schedule it into his schedule which was about 10 days out. When they did show up, they installed it in about 5 hours, start to finish. They called the Health Department and had it inspected before they covered it up and left. They were very efficient and got the job done quickly.

The engineering plan called for 12 piers to be buried 3 feet into the ground. They were 2 feet in diameter. So I needed 36 feet of 2 foot diameter sonotubes to pour the concrete into. I checked at Lowes and Home Depot, but they did not carry sonotubes that big. I ended up checking with a wholesale lumber supplier that deals with contractors. They did not carry them in stock but they could order them. So I ordered them. They came in 12 foot lengths, so I had them cut them into 3 foot sections for me. They cut them with a chain saw.

When I got the sonotubes home, I thought I could dig the holes for them by drilling some post holes and then cleaning out the remaining dirt with a shovel. After working for the whole day and only able to get the first hole down about 18 inches, I had to come to another plan. The ground was just too hard. I would use a crow bar for a while, then clean the hole out with a shovel. Then do it again. I could see that I was not going to be successful.

I came up with the idea to have a backhoe dig trenches three feet deep that I could put the sonotubes in. The trenches were symmetrical in each quadrant of the yurt, so I called and got a backhoe to come help me. In the photo you can see the trenches with the sonotubes laid down in them. You can also see the strings that divided the circle into quadrants.

After I set the sonotubes in the trenches, I positioned them and used stakes to stabilize them. Then I ordered concrete, according to the specifications in the engineering. I thought I should call the building inspectors and let them know I was going to pour. They came out and inspected the layout and how I was going to put the rebar into the piers. They signed off and I was ready to pour.

My son came and helped me pour the concrete. He works doing construction and knows a lot about pouring concrete. He has the vibrator to vibrate the concrete as it is poured into the sonotubes. This is very important and it is amazing to watch the concrete settle when the vibrator is put in the tube. It is important and required by the engineering.

One thing I learned was how important it is to have a good system for measuring and positioning the sonotubes accurately. In addition, positioning of the post caps into the concrete before it cures requires care and planning. I found the strings were not steady enough to really get good measurements. My son and I were trying to be real careful and get the post caps put in accurately with a measuring tape and the strings that marked the quadrants. I think if I were to do this again, I would build a 2x4 jig that would help me position the post caps accurately. The accurate positioning of the post caps translate into being able to be accurate with the beams which translates into being accurate with the platform.

I let the concrete piers cure for about 36 hours and got the backhoe in again to backfill the trenches. Then I put a sprinkler in place and let it run for a day or so. This settled the dirt and allowed me to add more dirt on top of the places that settled.

Next step was putting the 4x4 posts in place to support the beams. My property sloped about 7 inches over the 30 foot diameter of the yurt. I had to find out which pier was the lowest. Then I would make the post in that spot the longest one. Each post in the other piers would be shortened to make the whole platform level. I grabbed a 2x4 and my level and started to work. The more I measured and kept moving from pier to pier, the more confused I became. I would measure from one and then measure from another and get conflicting measurements. I was a bit frustrated. Along came my son to the rescue again.

He has a laser system that he loaned to me. These laser systems have a rotating laser on a tripod that you level up and turn on. The system has what is called a story stick. You put the laser detector on the story stick and move around until the detector starts beeping at you. It uses one set of beeps for being too low and another for being too high, so you can tell whether you are high or low. When you are right on, the tone is steady. The story stick has a measuring tape on it and you adjust the detector up and down until you get the steady tone and the stick is on the spot you want to measure. Read the tape and make your measurement.

I went around to each pier and measured how far it was from the level laser beam. This then told me which pier was the lowest. I put the first 4x4 post on that pier and set the height to the correct height for the platform. With that set, I knew exactly what I had to do at each pier to get the post to be the correct height. I went to each pier and measured, cut the post, installed it and moved on to the next pier. This system saved me a lot of time and it turned out to be very accurate. I highly recommend working with one of these systems to level up your platform.

The next step was to place the beams on the posts to create the structure to support the floor.

The picture shows me part way through putting the beams in place The plan called for using solid wood beams. If you are going to use those beams, you can't get them off the shelf. The lumber company had to order them from the mill and it would take about 6 weeks to get them milled and delivered. I waited too long before getting this going and I didn't have time to wait. Thus, I had to create the beams from 2x10's. I created the 4x10's by using two 2x10's to sandwich a ½ inch OSB board to give me the correct width. I created the 6x10 by nailing and screwing four 2x10's together. Lesson learned—plan further ahead.

Another lesson learned was that four of the posts supported 6x10 beams, yet the engineering called out for a 4x4 post. This created a problem at the top of the post where the beam was wider than the 4x4. The engineering called for adding thickness to the post to even out the width so that the Simpson brackets that held the beam to the post could be nailed on. I would have put a 6x6 post cap in the concrete and then the widths would have matched naturally. As a result, I ripped some 4x4 scraps to the right thickness to match to the thickness of the beams. It worked, but was just another adjustment that needed to be made.

The floor design was to sit on an octagonal set of beams. This was what the 6x10's created. On the angled set of 6x10's the engineering called for them to be square and to use some Simpson brackets to attach them. However, these brackets were not available in any of the stores, lumber stores, contractor wholesale lumber stores, quite literally—they weren't available, even from Simpson. So, I ended up mitering the ends, which in the end made a much stronger beam structure. The Simpson brackets that I used were 135 degree angle brackets.

The following picture shows the complete beam platform ready for the floor to go on next. This picture was taken October 28, 2013.

In the above picture you can see the yurt shipment sitting there covered with tarps. We were expecting rain in the coming few days.

I was concerned about the weather and having to put up my yurt in the cold and rain, or even snow at this time of year.

As I was working on the beams, I also started to get power ran to my yurt. I called Rocky Mountain Power and ordered new service. They sent an examiner out to look at my property and decide the best way to proceed. The examiner came out and explained the options to me and we decided what needed to be done. I had to get a meter panel installed according to the requirements. He left a booklet with me explaining exactly what needed to be done for the meter panel to be ready.

I had to buy the panel, get some conduit (3 inch grey PVC conduit) and the poly rope that is used to pull the wires through the conduit. I also needed a ground rod. It required that I dig a hole and pour a concrete pad around the support poles. It had to be 24 inches square, minimum. I went to work and got the panel installed at the edge of my property. This was 252 feet from the pole to my panel. Then I had another 130 feet to go from the panel to my yurt and the main breaker panel inside the yurt.

The conduit had to be buried 30 inches deep and I had to bore a hole under the road to get over to my side of the street. I called a contractor and he brought a crew out and we dug the trench and bored the hole and got the conduit over to the meter panel. Before I could call the power company and get them to come pull the lines, I had to get the panel inspected. I called the inspectors and they came right out and gave me the green light.

The power company only does new installations on Friday's. Don't ask me why. But I had to wait for two Friday's before they were able to come do my installation. It actually got pulled in and I got temporary power on November 5th.

I had to install some 2 inch conduit and a "#4 0 (ought) cable to the yurt. I hired a guy with a trencher to come dig both the power line trench 18 inches deep and the water line trench 60 inches deep.

I put the conduit to the yurt in one length at a time and fed the cable through it while I was installing it. This saved me from having to try to pull it through with a rope, as it is very stiff and bulky. This worked really well.

After putting the electrical line and the water line in, I backfilled the trenches and was ready to receive the shipment from Yurts.

I needed some help. With Dana's help at Rainier Yurts, I made arrangements with David Kirkhhof to come help me. David lives in northern Idaho on his property with six yurts on it. He is the guru of yurt builders. He has helped put up many yurts. He was scheduled to arrive on November 3rd, and we were going to put up the yurt in three days. He showed up on time and the construction process started the next day.

Here was the plan:

Day 1—Put the floor on the beams and complete the platform
Day 2—Put the walls up, install the rafters and the compression ring
Day 3—Put on the liner, insulation, and the outer cover, drying it in!

I needed some friends to help, so my son came to help, a local friend and his son helped, David and myself. So, we had a crew of 4 on Day 1 and Day 2. We had a crew of three on Day 3. A couple more people could have made it go faster, but that is what I had available to me.

I had ordered the SIP floor package. This is made up of Structural Insulated Panels (SIP). They are made up of two 7/16 OSB panels, one on top and one on the bottom with 5 ½ inches of rigid foam insulation between them. In the following picture you can see them.

They are cut to the right size at the factory and the process is very straight forward. They come with a drawing and are labeled with numbers like F1, F2,…. The drawing has you start in the middle with an F1 panel and then work out from either side by adding the panels according to the drawing and their number.

The panels are joined with a 2x6. So you put some glue on the foam, the upper and lower panels and fit a 2x6 into the recess. The 2x6 goes in so that half is in one panel and the other half is in the next panel. The panels are then screwed to the 2x6 with screws every 8 inches. This creates a nice strong seam.

In the above picture you can see the 2x6 in front of Gordon there. You can also see the label on the SIP panel. At the right, as it curves, you can see how the panels extend beyond the foam by a ways. This is where the 2x6's fit.

As you get all the panels in place, you have to wrap a 2x6 around the perimeter to fill the space between the top and bottom and the foam insulation. To do this, we cut some kerfs in the 2x6's, leaving about 3/8 inch uncut. These cuts then allowed the 2x6 to bend around the perimeter, giving a nice finish to the foam and to the edge of the platform.

In the above picture, my son is cutting the kerfs on the right as Gordon, David, and I install the rest of the floor.

At the end of Day 1 we had accomplished our goal. The platform was complete. The next picture shows the finished edge of the platform with the 2x6 mounted between the upper and lower OSB panels. Also this is the story strip wrapped around the platform and stapled in place.

The story strip is a great design feature of Rainier Yurts. It is a label that you wrap around the platform that tells you where everything is supposed to go. When you are putting up the lattice, you stretch it out until all the x's at the bottom line up with the x's on the story strip. That way you know it is stretched to the proper distance. In addition, each of the wall panels, insulation panels, rafters and door openings are all labeled in accordance with your specific yurt. The story strip represents the choices you made when ordering your yurt. The story strip really simplifies the construction process.

When we put the story strip on in the afternoon of Day 1, the back door that I had ordered, was lined up perfectly with the clean-out of the septic system. That was a problem. We surveyed the situation and I made the decision to rotate the story strip 55 inches counterclockwise. This resolved the problem. The total delay in making that decision was about 15-20 minutes, while we measured and verified everything else. With the yurt being round and the platform symmetrical, the impact was nothing really. In fact, later, the plumber said it improved the situation for him since it moved things away from one of the beams. So, the problem turned out to not be a problem at all.

Day 2 was a big day. We started by unpacking the two doors and setting them in place where the story strip showed they needed to be. They were supported by some 2x4's to hold them straight up and down while we continued to work.

The building code also required that I have a window that I can crawl out of in the bedroom, so I wouldn't be trapped in case of a fire. So we unpacked and installed the window, using the same method as for the doors.

While the doors were being installed, we unpacked the lattices. There were eight sections. They fold down to an amazingly small package. We laid them on the platform and began the assembly process of joining them together according to the instructions and the story strip. They were labeled A, B, C, etc. Going in a clockwise direction A, B, and C were bolted together. This section then stretched between the front door and the bedroom window. The window comprised section D. So sections E and F were bolted together and were stretched between the bedroom window and the back door. The rest were assembled and stretched between the back door and the front door.

The walls went up amazingly fast. The picture below is looking south at the backdoor. As the sections were put up, we attached the metal strips and screwed them into the platform. You can see them at the junction of the x's on the bottom of the lattice wall and the platform.

The next step was to put the tension cable in place on the top of the lattice wall and connect it together with the swaged ends and the clevis pin.

After putting the cable in place, the next step was to erect the scaffolding that was needed for the rafters and the compression ring. I had rented a 12-foot scaffold from a friend and we brought it in and got it set up. The scaffold allowed us to hold the compression ring in place while getting the rafters up to support it.

We had two people on the scaffold and two people on the platform that would hand the rafters up to the guys on the scaffold—who would insert the end into the compression ring and on the platform we would put the rafter in place and insert the cable into the slot in the end of the rafter.

One of the impressive safety features is the screw that locks the rafter onto the cable. We would have been in real trouble if while we were getting another rafter in place we would pull one that we already had in place free and it came falling down. The screw locks it in place and prevents injury. I was really pleased with that feature.

We put one rafter in each quadrant in place first, so that the compression ring was supported and then we systematically put the others in going from one side to the other to keep things in balance.

As you can see, as the sun was setting we completed the goal of Day 2, which was to have the frame completed.

The scaffolding is still in place as we will need it to install the insulation, cover and dome.

Day 3 started and we lost one member of our crew, so we only had 3 of us. We started folding and taping all the Reflective Barrier Insulation sections together. The wind was blowing a bit and this was sort of challenging to manage the taping while holding everything in place. The sections are joined with aluminum tape on both sides.

After taping the insulation, we put the liner on. It is the canvas lining that is visible from the interior of the yurt. On top of that we put the insulation.

In this photo, taken about 9 in the morning, David is checking the liner and insulation after we had put it up.

The next step was probably the most physically challenging of all the tasks that we performed. That is hoisting the top cover, made of 28 oz.

material, up onto the roof. It weighed about 175 lbs. and was bulky, as you might imagine. With one person on the scaffold, pulling on the rope and two of us down below lifting, we managed to get it started. After we got it started, one of us went up on top while one was holding from below. This was tough but within a few minutes we had it up there.

It is folded so that the outside surfaces are together inside the fold. That way when you pull it up, one of the inside surfaces is in the proper orientation. Once you get it up and spread out in a about a 180 degree span, then you full the top half over the top onto the other side and then it is completely in the correct orientation. After that, even it up and there you go! A roof in place!

By 11 am or so, the roof was up and we were ready to install the walls. Using the story strip and the packaged wall insulation panels, we put them on with jib hanks, hooking them to the wall cable sewn in the roof.

You can see that the yurt is really taking shape now. The walls go up just like the insulation. Just follow the story strip and the labels on the wall panels and hook them up to the wall cable.

To finish out Day 3, we lifted the dome up and secured it to the compression ring with the springs and the crank assembly that allows it to be opened for ventilation.

The day ended with a fantastic sunset. This was taken as a sign of approval!

Three days of hard work, about 9 hours each day and we had the exterior up and I was dried in. The weather could rain or snow, whatever, and I was going to be alright. It was a good feeling at the end of November 6, 2013.

CHAPTER 5

INTERIOR

Now that I was dried in, I needed to finish the interior. The first step was to frame in the bathroom. I had designed the floor layout so that the plumbing for the toilet, tub, bathroom sink and kitchen sink would all be in one wall. So I built the wall out of 2x6's so there would be room to get all the plumbing, water lines (hot and cold) into the wall. I was able to run the hot and cold lines under the platform for the tub, so that made it easy to get over to the other wall for the water heater, the washer and dryer.

As you can see, the tub is elevated and the lines are running under the platform. I asked myself how wide to make the bathroom. Well, the framing dimensions for the tub are 60.25 inches. So I made the walls 60.25 inches inside dimension. In the picture you can also see the backside of the main circuit breaker panel above the tub, facing away from the bathroom.

Notice that the vent is going out the side of the yurt. By doing this I don't have any holes in my roof. I measure the pipe at 1.5 inches and cut an x pattern in a 1.5 inch hole. Then I pushed the pipe in from the outside and grasped the four corners. I slid a 1.5 inch radiator hose clamp on the pipe and captured the four corners from the wall and secured them with the hose clamp, and put some silicone sealant on the outside. This made for a nice exit for the vent pipe. We put a 90 degree elbow on outside, pointing it down. Lots of worry but it went in so easy!

The whole bathroom is 60.25 inches wide by 12 feet long. The toilet is 15 inches from the tub and the vanity is 36 inches long. The black drain pipe turning away in the photo is the vanity sink drain and the one facing us in the photo is the kitchen sink drain.

The plumber used the PEX piping system, which is really slick. The red pipes are for the hot water and the blue pipes are for the cold water. The main shut off valve for the incoming water is in the wall under the bathroom vanity. You can see it in the photo. You can also see the metal conduit that goes down through the floor. This is the CFCI circuit for the water line heat tape that keeps the line from freezing.

In this photo is the bedroom frame. The bathroom is on the right side. On the left you can see the edge of the wood burning stove that is providing heat. Notice the nice natural light from the dome.

To frame the doors for the bathroom and the bedroom, the rough opening for a 32 inch door is 34 inches. Then when you put the pre-hung door in place, you can shim it to get it straight and level. When you buy the door, buy a shimming kit, which consists of several tapered boards that you can put in opposite each other and create a variable width shim.

Now, onto how I installed the wood burning stove. I bought a stove jack kit from Rainier Yurts and it comes with good instructions. Here is a quick overview. The kit consists of two sheet metal panels. One fits on the inside and the other fits on the outside. I cut the lattice as shown in the photo, by cutting out one X. Then I drew in the 12 inch circle and cut it all the way through both the insulation and the outer wall membrane. I had purchased a triple wall stovepipe T section. I put the T in so that one of the sides was down and the other side up. The down side becomes the clean out and the stove pipe attaches to the upper side.

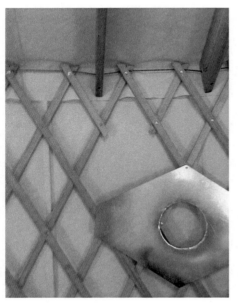

The piece that extends through the wall connects to the stovepipe through a 6 inch stovepipe adapter. The sheet metal is screwed into the lattice from the inside and the sheet metal on the outside is screwed into the lattice too. It has a section that extends up under the eaves of the roof, so it doesn't leak. Screw everything in place, using some self-tapping sheet metal screws.

To hold the chimney up, I dug a post-hole and planted a 4x4

pressure treated pole. It extended up alongside the triple wall stovepipe and supports it. They have some clamps that fit around the stove pipe and onto a cross member attached to the pole.

This photo shows the stove installed. I bent the 8 inch stove pipe into the oval shape to fit into the stove and left the other end round to fit into the adapter.

I also installed a propane gas stove to keep the place warm while I was away and the wood fire died down. I like the combination of both of them.

With heating taken care of, I will now discuss another of my questions. It is fairly standard with a range to have it connected to a 50 amp breaker (220 V). The dryer was standard at a 30 amp (220V) breaker. On both of these I used a 4 wire receptacle. The wiring is quite straightforward. The diagram is on the box that the receptacle comes in. Essentially, the red and black wires hook to the breaker; one wire to each of the terminals. The neutral goes to neutral and the ground to ground. This was not a difficult problem.

However, I couldn't find any information on the electric water heater. What I found out is that each water heater is rated for a certain size 220 V breaker. The documentation for the water heater will specify the size of the breaker. Also, there is not a plug or receptacle for the water heater. It is just wired directly from the breaker box into the water heater through a junction box and a flexible conduit. Mine was a 25 amp breaker and I wired it with 10 gauge wire.

Also, the electrical code requires an outlet every 10 feet along a wall. This is because most appliances come with a six foot cord and they don't want extension cords being used because of the fire danger. This was not a problem for the framed in walls in the interior, but for the circular outside walls of the yurt this presented a problem.

Do I go down through the floor and come up everywhere I need an outlet around the perimeter? That was one possibility. Another was bending metal conduit and attaching it to the floor all the way around with outlets spaced 10 feet apart.

Here is the solution I finally came up with. I used some plastic Wiremold conduit and the special outlet boxes they have for it. This conduit is used extensively in industry for wiring computers and networks. I found this at the wholesale electrical supply store.

Here is a picture of the part number information for the box.

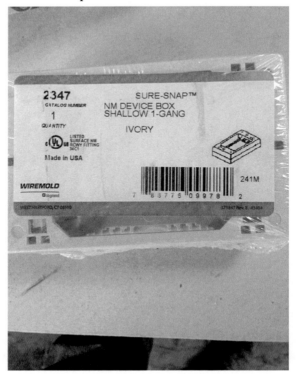

Another question I had was how to get the dryer vent outside. I got a stackable washer and dryer and I was wondering how hot it would be and would it create a leak path in the wall. In the end, I just got a lint trap and it stays inside and I didn't even go outside through the wall. Since I live in the desert here, and the woodstove heat is a dry heat, the moisture isn't a problem for me. Your conditions may vary.

This is a picture of my kitchen before the plumbing was completed and the upper cabinets installed. The kitchen is working well for me.

CHAPTER 6
LIVING IN MY YURT

What is it like living in my yurt? What have I learned so far? What would I do differently if I could do it again?

These are all good questions. First, what is it like? I love the dome and how it lets in so much light. It is great being in here during the day and the good light is very pleasant. I also love looking up out the dome to the night sky. I can see the stars and the moonlight coming in. It is a nice part of the yurt.

So far, it has been down to minus 20 degrees below zero. I have been warm. However, the temperature variation is more than living in a stick built home. The temperature in here usually varies between 58 to 75 degrees. I build a fire when I get up and the temperature is upper 50's or low 60's. I keep the thermostat for the gas stove at 67 degrees, usually. This keeps it pretty comfortable in here. The fire in the morning heats the place up and I work around here. The sun coming in brings the temperature up into the 70's and it is like this most of the day until around 4 pm, when the sun starts to set behind the mountain. Then I build another fire for the evening.

CHAPTER 6: LIVING IN MY YURT

When I go to bed, I put some wood on the fire and go to sleep. I usually wake up during the night to go to the bathroom and I put on a couple of more pieces of wood at that time. When I wake up, the fire in the stove has died out and the gas stove is on.

One thing that I learned that it is easier to put on thermal underwear than it is to burn a hot fire to keep the temperature in the 70's. So, I insulate myself and feel quite comfortable. In some countries in Europe where the homes don't have central heating, this is a common practice. It works!

I am burning about 20 six inch logs a day to stay warm and the temperatures have been in the single digits at night and low 20's during the day for the past month. We finally got a snow storm and the temperature hit the low 30's for the past few days. My wood usage went down!

I have a little electric infrared quartz heater in the bathroom that keeps it at 65 degrees. I love getting in the tub on the elevated platform. It is very comfortable in the bathroom.

I am sleeping well. It is surprisingly quiet inside, even compared to my small yurt. I enjoy peace and quiet. The birds wake me in the morning. My rhythm is natural, going to bed when it gets dark and getting up when it gets light.

I love my yurt.

What would I do different? There are some things I would change. One is that I would not divide the yurt in half with the interior walls again. The reason is that now it is difficult to access the full area of the dome. I can reach one half of it from the loft, but the other half is out over the living room and kitchen area. I would make my partitions so that it was completely accessible from the floor, or completely accessible from the loft.

Why is that important? Well, it relates to another lesson I learned. Having the wood stove over by the wall creates a hot side and a cold side of the yurt. It is harder to get the heat over to the cold side. Now the difference in temperature is not great, but it still is noticeable. I would rather have the stove centrally located so the heat spreads evenly from the center to the walls. This would mean taking the stovepipe up through the dome. That would mean replacing the dome with a dome that has the stovepipe accommodation. This solves two problems. One is getting the stovepipe high enough to have good draft, and two supporting it for high winds. A woodstove needs at least 15 feet to get a good draft. When going through the side, the 90 degree bends require the stovepipe to be longer to get the same draft. This is usually 3 feet for each 90-degree turn. This raises the stovepipe length to 21 feet.

Also, the more stovepipe that is inside the yurt, the more heat that is given off and not wasted. A stovepipe that goes up through the dome is at least 80% inside the yurt. This would improve heating quite a bit.

An example of a dome with the stovepipe through the center is from Nomad Shelters in Homer, Alaska. They have domes that do this with an octagonal shape with panes of Lexan to let in the light, and a triple wall stovepipe up the middle.

My stovepipe is not 21 feet and I don't think I can support it with the pole that I have. So I want to change my stove arrangement.

This is what is requiring me to want to access the dome. This is probably not a big issue for a three-season yurt. Where I am living in mine full time, and in a very cold climate, it is of a bigger issue for me. So take my learning here for what it is worth for you. The usage of your yurt will dictate how much you want to consider this.

Another thing that is interesting is the speed with which spiders create cobwebs in the rafters up near the dome. It would be much easier to clean them from the loft than the floor. So that is why I would change my layout a bit to accommodate the dome access. When visitors come, the first thing they look at is the dome. With the sun shining in, it highlights every single cobweb and gives me a little bit of embarrassment. I should have a clean yurt!!

Those are about the only things that I would do differently. I am so excited for spring so I can work on getting the deck done and the landscaping around the yurt completed.

Why is this yurt practical, as in the title of the book?

It is practical because living in a yurt is comfortable. In my yurt, I have included all the things that make a house comfortable. I have a refrigerator, a stove with an oven just like in the traditional house. I have a kitchen sink and cabinets just like a traditional house. I have a toilet, tub and sink in the bathroom, just like in a traditional house. My yurt is heated and comfortable in the winter. It has a bedroom with a walk in closet. I have a water heater, washer, dryer and freezer—just like a traditional house. For all practical purposes, I am living in a modern structure with all the conveniences.

Another factor that makes it practical is the lower cost of owner-ship. The yurt can be built on a budget. You don't have to have a large foundation. You could build a basement under the yurt if one wanted to increase the cost a bit. You can also elevate the yurt on columns to create a garage underneath the floor for parking and shop space. That would have to be engineered from a seismic viewpoint, but it is entirely possible. Others have done it.

Another idea, and I like this idea, is to build a community around the yurts, where there would be a central building with the laundry, bathrooms with showers, and that sort of common things, allowing the yurts to be more simple and less expensive. A yurt village. This idea would be great for an extended family.

Related to the above idea, is the idea of several small yurts erected in a circle around a central fire pit. Each yurt would have a specific purpose. The small yurt I built and used for a month, is an example. One yurt would be setup for a kitchen, another setup for a bedroom, another setup for guest entertainment, another setup for a shop space, another setup as a studio for writing, painting, and creative activities. Each with a small area to heat would be used as zone heating, thus only heated as needed. This could lead to some real waste reduction.

The large homes we live in traditionally, are in a certain sense, wasteful. Heating all the space we only occasionally use. Lighting all the space we only occasionally use. Many families do this by reminding the children to turn off the lights in the rooms that are not in use. However, a yurt with a specific purpose could easily be made to be efficient in this regard. Maybe, using yurts can instill as sense of simplicity to our lives. Do not have so much stuff to store. Live simple and frugal.

Many of the people who have come to visit my yurt, exclaim,

"This is beautiful!"

"I love the light from the dome."

"I love the wood"

One guy said, "This is certainly better than a single wide mobile home in terms of looks!"

The guy that came to deliver my firewood asked if he could take a picture of it! I said, "Yes, for a fee." This was after I asked him to stack the wood in the wood shed, whereupon he said, "Yes, for a fee." He took his pictures, inside and outside and we had fun teasing about the fees!

Ladies seem to be fascinated by the yurt. They come in and look around and start to talk about how they would arrange it, decorate it, etc. The guys come in and look at the cable and want to know about its strength, wind endurance, snow load, and they marvel at how well the parts all fit together. They almost universally say something along the lines of,

"This would make a great hunting cabin!"

My theory is that they aren't sure they could sell their wives on the idea, but they would sure like one sitting up in the mountains for their enjoyment. It is interesting to see the way they both interact after that initial exploration by both genders.

Is it beautiful? I think so.

I hope this has been helpful in answering some of your questions and making the planning process of your yurt easier and to reduce the amount of questions that keep you wondering all the time. I had fun building my yurt and I am enjoying living in it.

Good luck!!

Made in the USA
San Bernardino, CA
09 July 2017